Personalised page

Bonking
Roger's
Amazing
Dick,
Fills
Our
Requirements
Double-quick!

For Dennis
2009

'Nickers

Off

Ready

When

I

Come

Home

Jon Mountfort

Published by Luvbutton Press, Cambridge, England
a division of Luvbutton Ltd

www.luvbutton.co.uk

ISBN 978-0-9557635-0-2

2nd imprint October 2009

Copyright © Jonathan Mountfort 2007

The right of Jonathan Mountfort to be identified as the author of this work has been asserted by him in accordance with the Copyrights, Designs and Patents Act 1988.

All rights reserved.

Typeset by Luvbutton Press
Printed and bound in Great Britain by
Think Ink of Ipswich, Suffolk

Front cover illustration: Carrie by Steve Kingston
(reproduced with kind permission of the artist)

For all my friends at:

the Bedford Butterfly Park, Wilden
(now called Wild Britain)
and
The Lord John Russell, Public House, St Neots
and
also my bed

the three places where this book was mostly written

Introduction

The troops in the trenches during the Great War wrote various acronyms on the envelopes of their letters home to loved ones.

Some were sweet and poignant:

ITALY - I Trust And Love You
HOLLAND - Hope Our Love Lasts And Never Dies
and the very well known SWALK - Sealed With A Loving Kiss

especially as for many couples it would prove to be their last communication.

Others were of a more earthy, lustful nature:

EGYPT - Eager to Grab Your Pretty Toes (or any other T's you can think of)
BURMA - Be Undressed Ready My Angel
and CHIP (used presumably in the opposite direction) - Come Home I'm Pregnant!

But the most amusing of all of these had to be:

NORWICH - 'Nickers Off Ready When I Come Home

which is not only funny, but is also a town in England, which lead me to think, "could I make up some acronyms in reverse for other towns and cities in England, Scotland and Wales (and one for Northern Ireland)?"

So here is a trip around the British Isles, with a difference. In most cases I have tried to convey the essence of the places from which they are derived. In others I have taken the spirit of NORWICH and come up with epithets which are saucy and rude. For some places, you get both!

Cheers

Jon Mountfort
St Neots 2009

The route -
start and finish at Norwich

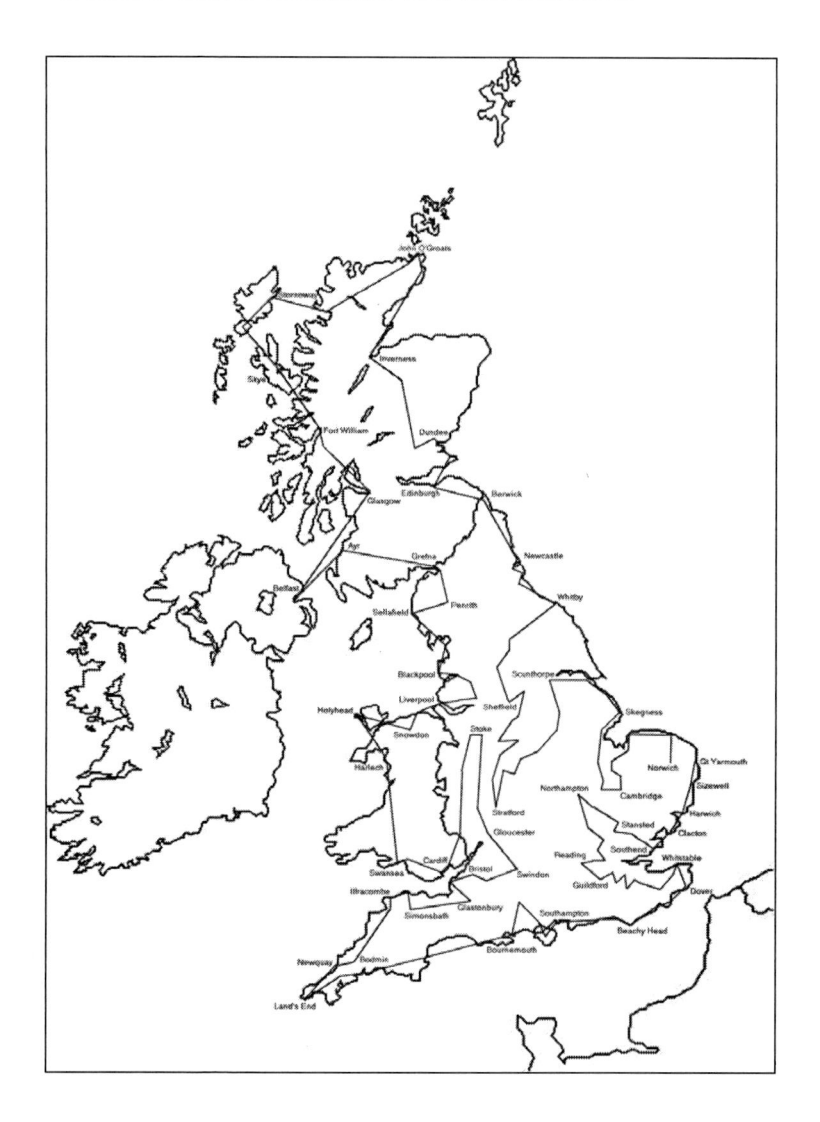

The places

All tours have to start somewhere and end somewhere. As the inspiration for this book is Norwich, I decided that we shall both start and end our trip around the British Isles in that city. Hence, with another popular epithet for NORWICH in our minds:

    Name
     One
      Reason
     Why
       I
        Came
         Here **!!**

we leave as quickly as possible and head for the picturesque and quaint seaside towns that dot the north Norfolk coast.

One particular town is especially famous for its crustaceans. But this needn't be a drawback. Provided one chooses partners carefully and takes the elementary precautions advertised in NHS leaflets,

    Crabs
   Rarely
  Overwhelm
 My
  Erogenous
   Regions

Cromer used to have a rock out to sea - Church Rock. When a ship struck it in 1888 it was blown up and now does not reveal itself even at low tide. I expect that made a few crabs homeless.

Moving on westwards, another delightful spot provides entertainment of a dark and slippery kind:

  Seals
 Happily
 Enjoy
  Repose
 In
  Numbers,
   Granting
    Holiday-makers
   Audiences
    Magnanimously

Apparently, as the place has no harbour, the Sheringham lifeboat had to be launched by tractor. "Hold on a minut there me ol' booty - don't drown till I'm ready - I just gotta start me tractor! Hev you seen the starten hendle?"

Further along the coast is the place where the archaeologists ripped Seahenge from where it had stood for thousands of years and now can't make up their minds what to do with it:

    Historic
   Old
  Log
   Monument
    Emerges

      Nautically
     E
      Xposed,
       Then

        Three
        Hundred
        "Experts**"**

          Suggest
          Extraction
          Archaeologically

Sacrilege! Another even older timber circle has been discovered 100 metres east of the site of the first. Known as Holme II, it dates to 2400-2030 BC and has been left in situ, probably because of the controversy over the removal of Holme I which is moving to King's Lynn.

One of the loveliest old towns on the north Norfolk coast actually faces west. This is interesting because, along with Heacham, it is the only place on the east coast of Britain where you can watch the sun set into the sea. It is therefore a place which

      Hosts
      Unusual
      Nautical
       Sunsets
       That
        Attractively
       Nuzzle
       The
       Ocean
       Nightly

Hunstanton is also noted for its cliffs with amazing bands of red (iron oxide) and white (chalk) like a candy stick.

We head south now and into Cambridgeshire where we find a large fen town, notable for its brewery (Elgoods - my mate is the head brewer!) and all the wealth and variety of crops grown in the low flatlands around it. For this reason, the headline in the local newspaper might read:

    World-wide
     International
      Sugar
     Beet
      Exhibition
     Clogs
      Hotels

Then again, it might not. Wisbech had the first canning factory in Britain - how did they open them? No-one had a tin-opener in those days. The little train which brought all those fruits and vegetables from the farms to the factory was pulled by a tram engine. During the 1950s, the Reverend W Awdry was Vicar of Emneth, a village near Wisbech. He saw the little train every day and called the engine "Toby". The real train has gone, but you can still walk into any toy shop and buy Toby the Tram Engine today.

Another Cambridgeshire fen town famous for its vegetables is also famous for being a "month". If you wish to sample the local knobbly orange produce for which it is renowned, then I'll offer you this

> **M**asturbation
> **A**dvice **:**
>   **R**aw
>   **C**arrots
>   **H**urt

A better tip is - only use the tip. If in doubt, refer to the next entry ...

... which is the most striking fen conurbation of all. It has an amazing cathedral but unfortunately only three letters, none of which is a "C". For this reason, we shall perform a logical leap from the previous town and announce the obvious fact that

> **E**els
> **L**ubricate
>   **Y**ou

On this was based the origin of the name Ely - it was the Isle of Eels !

It used to be an Isle indeed, with deep and dangerous swamps all around, hence the cathedral was christened "The Ship of the Fens". But now, with the land drained, it is simply a hillock in the middle of a plain.

There are lots of rumours about the fen folk - I know because I live in Cambridgeshire. Some remember the time when

    Cliff
      Hijacked
   A
      Tractor
     To
       Elope
        Round
       'Is
         Sister's

It is said, perhaps unkindly, that the only virgins around here are girls who can run faster than their brothers.

Which brings us to another den of iniquity where:

> **C**loistered
>   **A**cademics
>   **M**eet
>   **B**eefy
>   **R**owers
>   **I**n
>   **D**egree-
>   **G**iving
>   **E**xperience

In the old days of course it was full of painters, poets and pederasts. I'm sure things must have changed... or have they?

> **C**lawing
>   **A**t
>   **M**atron's
>   **B**ath
>   **R**obe
>   **I**nduces
>   **D**irty
>   **G**reat
>   **E**rection

A mere 16 mile chug westward and we arrive at my home town, the town in which I was born, so I shall praise it by saying:

Superb
Town

Near
Eynesbury
Offers
Top
Sex

Eynesbury is a little village attached to St Neots (it was actually there first so many residents would argue that St Neots is attached to Eynesbury) and is where my mother-in-law lives. I could do one for Eynesbury, but for this reason I'd better not.

St Neots church is very big for a parish church. It is almost a cathedral. Roger the vicar* (a name not an invitation) flies the flag of St George from its tower. You won't be able to do that soon - it will be illegal. (What - fly a flag? or Roger the vicar?)

*Roger no longer the vicar - as he has since retired.

The place which everyone in St Neots hates more than any other is the:

    Horriblest,
     Ugliest,
      Naffest
       Town...
        It
         Needs
          Gutting,
           Demolishing!
          Order
           Nitro-glycerine

which is just 9 miles to the north and the old county town of Huntingdonshire, now subsumed into the blandness of Cambridgeshire and only notorious for being the birthplace of Oliver Cromwell. But Huntingdon still has the District Council which rules the roost and spends all the money on itself and not on us - a situation of petty local envy which must be repeated in numerous places up and down the country.

A further 20 miles or so north and we arrive at a place that's so boring I am stumped.

Er...

Um...

I'll just make a cup of tea...

Er...

Ah... got it !!

    Penning
    Epithets
   That
     Encapsulate
    Rather
    Boring
    Ordinary
    Regions
     Observantly,
      Undoubtedly
     Gets
     Harder

This happens to be true. What can you say about Peterborough? It has a lovely cathedral which interestingly has some 17th century graffiti carved into its pillars - in this case slogans left by Cromwell's republicans. But other than that, Peterborough is quite tedious.

Heading north into Lincolnshire and east a bit, back to the coast, I'm stumped again by a church tower that is so tall that the

> **B**ig
>   **O**ld
>   **S**teeple
>   **T**ook
>   **O**n
>   **N**ickname

At 272 feet high with no pointy bit on top, it's affectionately known as the "Boston Stump". We'd like to know the real reason it got its nickname, but it seems it's not just me - everyone's stumped on this one. Perhaps it was actually the Boston *Stomp* - a dance performed to shake the claggy fenland soil from work boots.

Perhaps it could also be that this

> **B**iggest
> **O**f
>   **S**tumps
>   **T**hrills
>   **O**ctogenarian
>   **N**uns

Following along the north shore of the Wash and then turning left, we arrive at a beach. A very long beach. A very well known long beach where

> **S**wim-suited
> **K**ids
> **E**njoy
> **G**ames
> **N**ear
> **E**ndless
> **S**andy
> **S**ea

When the weather's nice it's a lovely place (so I'm told). The advertising blurb designed by John Hassall for the Great Northern Railway used a picture of the "jolly fisherman" and the famous slogan "Skegness is so bracing" which is a lovely line in understatement. He must have meant the "double-pneumonia" kind of bracing. (What is double-pneumonia? Does anyone know anyone who's had it? Or do two people have to get it?)

Turning northwards, the coast stays sandy all the way, but the North Sea in a gale is still treacherous and:

    Many
   A
     Blessed
      Lifeboatman
       Embarks
        To
         Help
          Others,
           Risking
            Personal
             Extinction

Now that we have lifeboat *women*, I wonder if any of them are called Gail?

Before we head inland, the air gets fishier, and on the seamen's days in port:

    Girls
     Rebuff
      Inebriated
       Mariners
        Spinning
        Boring
         Yarns

Grimsby dock tower must be the tallest water tower in the universe. It was built in 1867 to provide hydraulic power to operate the lock gates and cranes of Grimsby docks. It is 309 feet high - 37 feet more than Boston Stump - so I make it that the water pressure at the bottom must be around 135 pounds per square inch. It is supposedly built on foundations of cotton wool. This legend came about because the engineers used wool bales to soak up the last drops of water which they had trouble pumping out of the workings.

A short trip to the west brings us to a place where a

> **S**eemingly
> **C**ourteous
> **U**nremarkable
> **N**orthern
> **T**own
> **H**ides
> **O**bscenely
> **R**ude
> **P**opular
> **E**xpletive

which I cannot possibly repeat here. We'll just say that "Net-Nanny" might not let you access the local tourist information centre website.

Without dallying, let us now head to the county town where, atop a column inside the cathedral, at the apex of two vaults,

    Lincoln's
     Imp
      Naughtily
       Crouches
        On
         Limestone
          Niche

Apparently, two imps were indeed very naughty one day, one even managing to trip up the bishop - although how this was accomplished we can only imagine. Luckily an angel was around to sort things out, turning one imp to stone and allowing the other to escape, presumably so it could report back to the Devil that it wasn't worth imping around in Lincoln as the consequences were petrifying. New imps are recruited using an advert in the paper:

Lissom
  Impish
   Nymph-like
    Coquettish
    Old
     Ladies
      Needed

Another Lincolnshire town was unheard of to 99% of the British population until 1979 when a certain person became the first PM to have ever experienced PMT.

Grocers
 Release
  A
   Nationwide
    Time-bomb:
    Historic
     Action-girl
      Margaret !

Margaret Hilda Thatcher is loved, admired, hated and denigrated in equal measure - but at least she kept the electric on while we were cooking the Christmas turkey. Do you remember the days when every household had a shoe-box full of candles and a box of matches? You never knew whether you'd see the end of Coronation Street before another power cut.

Our next stop is the putative home of pork pies - which is a shame really because, despite having many constituent letters, there is not one "P" amongst them.

    Missing
    Essential
    Letter
    To
    Outline
    Noted

    "**M**eat
    Occupying
    Wheat"
    Begets
    Rather
    Ambling
    Yarn

Just how do you get a reference to "pork pie" into Melton Mowbray? This is my best shot...

Now let's go on a trip around the Midlands. One of these towns must be the furthest from the sea of any town in Britain, but I don't know which one. Maybe it's the place whose

    Largest
     Export
      Is
       Crisps,
        Expanding
         School-kids
          Tummies
           Enjoying
            Ready-salted

What does Leicester mean to you? Cheese? Rugby Union? Crisps? Or some bloke with big ears? But I bet you didn't come up with "the first roundabout in the UK".

Talking about a game with 15 fat blokes stamping on each others' knackers, they're just

    Rough
    Ugly
     Great
      Bullies
       Yelling

until they get in the bar afterwards - then they're all pussycats.

A good place for rugby players to form a scrum to secure a front row view would be our next famous city where, a long time ago, we would have seen

    Crowds
     Of
      Visitors
       Eyeing
        Naked
         Titties
          Rhythmically
         Yo-yoing

(in my dreams) which of course would be dreams of Lady Godiva who, if she ever existed, needed a damn-good haircut. (You thought I was going to say "seeing-to" then, didn't you!)

If you did manage to get a peek at the noble norberries and you got caught, you probably spent a few days in...... Coventry...... (oh dear!)...... There, while in enforced solitude, you could send out for a good yarn written just down the road.

Shakespeare's
  Town
   Really
    Attracts
     Tourists
    For
     Obvious
      Reasons…
     Does

        Ultimate
        Playwright
        Offer
        Noisy

          Americans
          Value
          Or
          Not **?**

And so to England's "second" city which, unless you live there, is vaguely anonymous.

It's only

    Because
   I
    Read
     Maps
     I
      Notice
       Great Britain
       Has
      A
       Middle

Strange place Birmingham - no one goes there unless they're forced to by their boss (endless boring trade exhibitions at the NEC), or the M6 is shut.

Someone should tow it off a hundred miles to the left (to mid-Wales where there's absolutely bugger-all) and free up the motorways which all converge on Birmingham and get stuck. It's like someone in the Ministry of Transport sat down with a map and a pen in the 1960s and said, "Let's design a traffic jam."

Now to a place which was seminal in the enjoyment of one of my favourite hobbies.

> **B**rewers'
> **U**llage
> **R**educes
> **T**elescopic
> **O**rgans
> **N**o-end

and after a night in the pub you feel like you've been

> **B**uying
> **U**mpteen
> **R**ounds
> **T**o
> **O**thers'
> **N**one

At one time there were 37 breweries in Burton-on-Trent (I just made that up but it sounds about right). Now I think there are around two.

William Bass established a brewery in Burton-on-Trent in 1777, and you can still buy the stuff. And it's good too.

Next, we're off to a place of legend, and the inspiration for a thousand Hollywood movies and British television series, where once a:

    Notorious
     Outlaw
      Told
       Tuck -
    "I
        Nearly
         Got
          Hitched !
         Ask
          Marian"

A lucky escape among many lucky escapes, as this particular

    Super
     Hero
      Enjoyed
       Redistributing
       Wealth
      Of
       Others
        Daringly

To round off our tour of the Midlands, a skirmish with the Peak District is called for, with all its stark beauty, lovely dialects and skinny blokes wearing hard-hats with lamps on and ropes round their middles who are

    Modelling
   A
    Tatty
   Load
  Of
    Caving
   Kit

These are potholers. In potholes, you generally find water. And the water is very cold, and very clear, and very minerally. In fact it is

  A
   Super
  H$_2$O
   Born
  Of
    Underground
   Rocks,
    Naturally
     Effervescent

Therefore, to base an industry on the stuff is an extremely good idea. But I want to drink mine before those potholers have splashed their bollocks around in it.

Head north again and we arrive at the most famous architectural cock-up in Britain - a bit like Pisa's leaning tower I suppose, but pointier.

Can't
Help
Enjoying
Sensational
Twisted
Erection,
Rising
Fluted
In
Ever
Lessening
Diameter

Chesterfield's twisted spire was never intended to be that way (just like Pisa's tower was never meant to topple over) - it's just that the timbers warped. A legend says that one day a virgin got married in the church and the spire bent down to get a closer look. I wonder why they haven't asked the builders for a quote to straighten it?

From a place with a remarkable feature to one with virtually none (unless you count the Oxo factory). But never mind, just remember that after she has her 'Nickers Off Ready,

> **W**ise
>   **O**perators
>   **R**arely
>   **K**iss
>   **S**cratchy
>   **O**ld
>   **P**ussies

A mate of mine from round this area told me Worksop had good chip shops. "Eh oop... nah then... you can't beat a Worksop chip-'ole..." as he put it.

Further north of Worksop is a town that was, at one time, mainly an engine shed and workshops (Worksops?).

> **D**eafening
>   **O**ver-
>   **N**ight
>   **C**lamour
>   **A**s
>   **S**team
>   **T**rains
>   **E**xpertly
>   **R**epaired

24 hours a day, 7 days a week they smashed and bashed and shovelled and steamed. If only it was still like that now...

A hop to the left (that's left on my map) and we're in a place that once had a steel industry - well it may still do for all I know.

    Steel
     Honed
      Especially
       Finely
       For
        Implements
        Embodying
         Lasting
          Dependability

But what you can still do in Sheffield is

    See
     Heaven
     Each
      Friday...
      Fiona
     Is
      Every
       Lad's
        Dream

Near Sheffield is a place where, once, when

    Rolling
   On
  To
   Hannah**,**
    Eddie
     Remembered
    His
     Animal
      Magic

Carrying on up through Yorkshire (we'll by-pass Lancashire for now and do it on the way back south) we come to a place which is a melting-pot of cultures and accents.

   Bollywood
   Recreated
  As
   Dreams
   Flicker
   Onto
    Recordable
   DVDs

I love hearing Indians and Pakistanis with Yorkshire accents. The Birmingham ones sound great too... And the Scottish... And the Welsh...

Even further north and, briefly, we get posh - it has recently been named the UK's 3rd best place to live. On the Party Conference circuit, this is the place where:

Having
 A
  Relaxing
  Reefer
  Once
  Got
  A
   Tory
   Expelled

whereas:

Having
 Adulterous
  Rumpy-pumpy
  Really
   Often,
    Guarantees
   A
    Title ...
     Eventually

Keeping on going to a place where

>**R**acing
>**I**s
>**P**ostponed
>**O**ver
>**N**obbling

we head for the sea again and somewhere in which can be had a real North Yorkshire pint and a pie and a bucket of sand. Unfortunately, while walking along, minding you own business, a

>**W**ire
>**H**aired
>**I**rritable
>**T**errier
>**B**ites
>**Y**ou

You know the one I'm talking about! It's only got one eye. The dogs in Yorkshire are very cantankerous - they take after their owners.

Continuing north, we are now surrounded by places famous for propelling the country into the industrial age, one of the most important being where

Stephenson's
Tracks
Overcame
Canals,
Killing
Tired
Old
Narrow-boats

Contrary to popular myth, the Stockton and Darlington (1825) was definitely not the first railway (no-one knows which was the first British railway - wooden tracks were used in mines all over the country), nor was it the first steam railway (this was possibly Middleton Colliery Railway 1812), nor even was it the first railway to carry passengers (Swansea to Oystermouth 1807). Neither was it the first railway which, as a public right of way, was built after obtaining an Act of Parliament to sanction its construction (this was the Surrey Iron Railway from Wandsworth to Croydon 1801). All we can safely say is that it was the first railway designed from the start to use steam locomotives, and the first which had purpose-built stations (one at either end). Mostly it was used for hauling goods - the number of passengers carried was very small and the carriages were still hauled by horses. The first "proper" railway as we would come to know it was the Liverpool and Manchester (1830) - see RAINHILL.

Our next town is on the seaside once more and carries its own myth about which the locals are rather sensitive.

    Hanging
     Apes
      Rouses
       The
        Loud
         Excitable
          Passions
           Of
            Orang-utan
             Lovers

It is said that during the Napoleonic wars the locals watched a French vessel founder and then waited for anything that was washed up on shore. The only survivor was a poor monkey, dressed in a French military uniform. They questioned the monkey, ascertained he was a spy and hanged the poor creature in the town square, hence people from this area are now called "monkey hangers".

The county town around here is a place which I thought was really old, but apparently dates from as late as 1000AD. Some northern traditions are more ancient however:

    Damp
     Undies
      Ritually
       Hung-out
        Around
         Mondies

There's a wonderful cathedral where the Venerable Bede is buried. I should like to be remembered as Venerable when I peg out, but I somehow think a different adjective will be found to describe my talents. Venerial Bleed? Or Vulgar Bleeder maybe?

Back on the theme of industrialisation, most of our industry has now gone abroad:

    Clapped
   Out
  Noisy
   Smelters
    Exported
   To
    Taiwan

Consett was a vast iron and steel production line with huge railway sidings and lots of smoke and steam. Now it's a Tescos car park. It's bollocks really isn't it...

The only heaving, living, never-sleeping town left around here is that great big one on the Tyne where they have

   Nightlife -
    Entertainment -
   Wild
    Clubbing -
    A
     Solution
     To
      Life's
       Ennui

which reminds me

>**W**hy
>　**A**re
>　　**L**arge
>　　**L**adies
>　　　**S**uch
>　　　　**E**nchantingly
>　　　　**N**imble
>　　　　　**D**ancers?

You can party away all your troubles, or you can journey with us ever more northward to where the pace of life is like a 20-zone compared with a motorway. We're heading for Scotland, but:

>**B**efore
>　**E**ngland
>　**R**ecedes
>　**W**e
>　　**I**nsulate
>　　　**C**lothes &
>　　　**K**nickers

because it's always flipping freezing up in Caledonia. From Berwick it's just a skip and a trip to the border (I know because I skipped then tripped over the border after too many ales).

The capital is one of my favourite places where we

      Eat,
       Drink,
        Imbibe
         Nine
          Beers,
           Urinate,
          Rant,
          Get
            Hammered

Did you know that the rock on which the castle stands is actually the plug of solid lava solidified in the centre of an extinct volcano? The actual conical volcano bit has all been dissolved away by the incessant Scottish rain, leaving just the hard bit which blocked up the blow-hole after it fired for the very last time. And when would that be? Say around 300 million years ago. And how long ago is that? Let's try to imagine. Say your local mediaeval church is 1000 years old from the time it was built, you could have built three hundred thousand of them in the time since the volcano last erupted. No - that's still unimaginable - I give up.

Across the awesome Forth Bridge (either one of them) and to the right a bit and we come to the home of golf where

    Severiano
    Takes

      A
     New
      Driver,
       Raises
        Elbows,
         Whacks ......
        Sand **!**

Before 1878, we would have had to take a ferry to get to our next port of call. Then, for 18 months, we could have done it in the (sort-of) comfort of a Victorian railway carriage. Then we were back to the old ferry again for seven and a half years - until July 1887 to be precise.

This hiatus was caused by the fall of the first Tay Bridge, when a

Dismally
  Unpleasant
   Night
    Drowned
   Errant
    Engine

Everyone was killed (around 75) and this was the only railway accident in Britain to have killed everyone on board. The engine however was a survivor. Despite resisting two attempts at salvage, at the third try it was returned to dry land and repaired. Nicknamed "The Diver", for years no driver would take her across the new bridge, but on December 28th 1908, the twenty ninth anniversary of the collapse, it passed safely over the second Tay Bridge. The piers of the first still stick from the water like stumps of rotten teeth, a reminder of what can go wrong.

We'll saunter across westwards now to the southern gateway to the Highlands where rufty-tufty Scotsmen play rufty-tufty games all year round without any underwear on. The most elementary of these games is "tossing the caber":

    Pole
     Erect.
      Ready **?**
     Toss
      Hard ...

It's flipping a telegraph pole over on its end and hoping it won't fall back on top of you.

Many many miles north now and we're in the centre of the snowboarding universe where

    Amateur
     Venturers
      Ignominiously
       Escape
        Mountains
         On
          Rescue
          'Elicopter

That's me!

Norther and norther and, take a deep breath...

aaaaaaaaaaaaaaaahhhhhhhhhh...

suck in that cold but invigorating Scottish air we're in monster-territory.

> **I**s
>   **N**essie
>   **V**anished
>   **E**vermore **?**
>   **R**emember
>   **N**ot
>   **E**veryone's
>   **S**o
>   **S**ure **!**

Inverness is a magnet for bagpipe players and every September they hold a competition. Is this what attracts Nessie from the depths of his Loch? No, I doubt it either.

Norther and still norther, someone actually built a railway line up here! What's more, it's still open! Isn't that amazing? They've closed lines like those to Ilfracombe and Hunstanton where people actually go, and they've left this one open. Not that I'm knocking it - I'm truly happy that it's still here - it's just a shame about the others.

This line splits near the end and goes to two places: one where you can

    Wade
     In
      Cold
       Kelp

and the other where, hopefully, the

    Train
     Halts,
      Ultimately
       Reaching
        Scotland's
        Outpost

If it doesn't then it's in the drink, for from here we can't go any further north unless we swim, but if any birdwatchers would care to

    Jump
     Overboard
      Heading
       North,

          Observe

Gulls
Round
Orkney,
Auks,
Terns,
Skuas

Now we'll trundle off south west to the place where you can catch a ferry to the Outer Hebrides.

There is something sad and romantic about this part of the world. An

Unworldly
Lament
Lingers
As
Port
Our
Oarsmen
Leave

It must be the memories of all those battles and escapes from feuding clans - not to mention the terrible English of course.

We now hop on the ferry. The Isle of Lewis has a strong church and strict rules, even these days, and in its one decent sized town, the

      Sunday
       Trading
        Opponents
         Repeat :
        "**N**
         O
          W
           A
            Y"

They even got funny about the ferry running on a Sunday. The only way I found to spend a penny on a Sunday was in the bog (Scottish peat bog that is).

If we head south, we can

      Have
     A
       Right
        Romp
         Impregnating
          Sheep

The Isle of Harris is joined to Lewis, which I find a bit odd, as from the names you would think they were individual islands separated by water. The Isle of Lewis is mostly flat and covered in sheep. Harris is mostly mountainous and covered in sheep. The road around the south of Harris defines a circular path around a landscape which I can only describe as lunar, but with sheep. It is quite breathtaking and well worth a visit.

Back on another ferry and we arrive at that most evocative and well-known Scottish island of all, which was the scene of a

      Scottish
      King's
      Yacht
      Escape

Have you ever been seduced by the Cuillins? No but I'd like to be. They're mountains by the way.

After taking yet another ferry to Mallaig, we chug south (chugging is as fast as you can go around here) to the capital of the West Highlands.

Facing
  One-side:
    Rising
     Tide

      While
      Inland
       Looming
       Large:
        Inverlochy's
        Amazing
        Mountain

which is "Ben Nevis". Until the 18th century there was no Fort William - just the nearby village of Inverlochy. The "fort" was installed by Cromwell to subdue the Jacobite uprisings and the town which grew around it was subsequently named after William of Orange. The Scots have been intending to change its name to a less contentious one for years, but have not yet got around to it.

South of Fort William lies another famous place with a dark history where if you've

> **G**ot
>   **L**oud
>   **E**xcitable
>   **N**eighbours**?**
>   **C**ampbells
>   **O**ffer
>   **E**xtermination

It's the thanks you get... I mean... you offer your guests full-board - they get dinner and bed, then eat you for breakfast.

The best way to forget about those troubled times past is to understand that

> **G**uzzling
>   **L**ager
>   **A**nd
>   **S**inging
>   **G**laddens
>   **O**ur
>   **W**eekend

Yes - that's my kind of town! They also build ships on the Clyde, so with that in mind, we'll nip across the Irish Sea to a

Birthplace's
Everlasting
Lament
For
A
Ship :
Titanic

Titanic was constructed in the Belfast shipyard of Harland and Wolff from 1909 to 1912. A lot of effort for just one voyage, but they did get ice in their drinks.

Returning to Scotland again on the next ferry, we pass through

All
Year
Rain

This is where Robert the Bruce held his first Scottish parliament, in St John's Tower by the sea. I hope it didn't have a leaky roof.

Before crossing the border back into England, we stop off to attend a service for some

> **G**iddy
>   **R**omancers
>   **E**loping
>   **T**o
>   **N**uptial
>   **A**ssignation

before they head quickly off to their next appointment: a quickie divorce, perhaps in a place where they **R**outinely **E**nd **N**uptial **O**bligations.

England's frontier outpost was, at one time, teeming to the sound of railway engines from about eight different railway companies and three separate railway stations.

> **C**aressing
>   **A**
>   **R**egulator,
>   **L**etting
>   **I**n
>   **S**team,
>   **L**ocomotive
>   **E**rupting

we charge up the hill, our

> **S**teaming
> **E**xpress
> **T**aking
> **T**wo
> **L**ight
> **E**ngines

to haul it up the "long drag" to Ais Gill summit and then down the other side to settle in Settle. There was a famous case of "two light engines" on Christmas Eve 1910. In railway parlance, a "light" engine is one which has nothing behind it - no carriages or trucks. The light engines were used to assist the heavily laden expresses from Carlisle, pushing them up to the top of the hill. They were then detached, turned round on the turntable at Hawes Junction, and waited to run back down the hill to Carlisle. On this occasion, the signalman forgot they were there and cleared the signals for an express coming from the south. The two light engines sauntered off north at a leisurely pace, the express soon caught them up, and WALLOP...! The wreckage caught fire and nine people died.

The other route south out of Carlisle by train is up another hill to Shap summit. If you look out of the carriage window just before you reach the top, you may see

    People
     Enjoying
      Naked
       Romps
        In
         The
          Hills

If you could see across the hills, to the coast, you will find a giant industrial complex, built in the 1940s/50s to produce plutonium for Britain's atom bomb, which is still to this day:

    "**S**afely"
     Emitting
      Low-
       Level
        Atomic
         Fallout
          In
           Ever
            Larger
             Doses

Unless of course you ask the politicians...

Trundling down into Lancashire, we arrive at vast sandflats where you can, if not careful, become

    Marooned
     On
      Ridge
       Excavating
      Cockles
     And
       Mussels
      Before
       Eventide

But should you need cheering up, just look at the statue of Eric (as in Morecambe) which is on the seafront.

Hurtling down the coast and on the same theme, we find that

    Feeling
   Lucky,
  Eric
   Entertains
    Two
     Well-
    Off
    Old
     Dears

Our next town is the most famous in the land for

    Bright
     Lights
    And
      Cheeky
       Kisses,
      Plenty
      Of
      '**O**liday
        Laughter

You'll see loads of

    Bums
    Legs
    And
     Colossal
      Knockers,
       Postcards
      Of
        Overlarge
        Ladies

It is noted for its illuminations, one of which is

>**B**lack
>**L**acy
>**A**rse-
>**C**rack
>**K**nickers
>**P**eeping
>**O**ut
>**O**ver
>**L**eggings

The illuminating thing about this particular observation is, if the thong's damp at the bottom then it's sunny, if the thong's damp at the top then it's raining. Simple when you know how.

Off to the administrative centre of Lancashire where

>**P**rostitutes
>**R**oam
>**E**mpty
>**S**treets
>**T**aking
>**O**rders
>**N**ightly

Moving swiftly on, we're now in the midst of the great cotton and weaving revolution of the 18th and 19th centuries. There's none of this industry left now though:

    Remember
     Our
      Cotton
       Has
        Disappeared
         And
          Leaves
           Echoes

Echoes of Gracie Fields, maybe, who was born here.

Another startling invention occurred in these parts when

    Millers
     Arranged
      National
       Competition -
      Hovis
       Emerged
        Supreme -
       Toast
        Entirely
         Revolutionised

The process of producing long-lasting and tasty wheatgerm flour was perfected by Richard "Stoney" Smith in 1886. It was first marketed as Smith's Patent Process Germ Flour. There had to be a better name, so a competition was organised to find it. This was won by a London student called Herbert Grimes who derived the name Hovis from the amalgamation of two Latin words - "hominis vis" meaning "strength of man". Grimes appears never to have benefited from his triumph, but after his death the grateful company paid his widow a pension. He obviously needed an agent.

While still on the subject of flour, what about those pastries where

    Each
     Cake
      Contains
       Lousy
        Eight
         Sultanas

It's a great name for a cake though - once heard never forgotten.

We quickly skirt round a place where, if all the reality police TV programmes are to be believed, is the epitome of

Scum
  And
    Low-life,
      Full
        Of
          Rapist
            Druggies

and zoom across to a town famous for its rugby league team. But it has neither "R" nor "L" in its name, nor even "U" for an "up-an-under" so we have to ask a more fundamental question:

What
  Is
    Good
      About
        Northerners **?**

Don't take it personally - I'll take the piss out of southerners later.

Just south of Wigan is the place where

Rocket
  Attained
    Immortality,
   Nimbly
    Hauling
     Its
       Largest
      Load

The Rainhill trials of October 1829 were organised to decide whether or not self-propelled steam locomotives were powerful enough and reliable enough to haul trains on the Liverpool and Manchester Railway which, at the time, was under construction. It was the first inter-city railway line in the world. Its backers wanted a return on their money and it was still a possibility that it would end up being horse powered, as many doubted that the added cost of locomotives would be justified. Rocket proved they could do the job and when the line opened on September 15th 1830 it was locomotive hauled for almost its full distance. Rocket was once again in the news on this day for it ran over the local MP William Huskisson, crushing his leg. He was rushed to the vicarage at Eccles (perhaps they thought they'd cut out the doctor/hospital scenario and go straight for the vicar/last rites) where he died a few hours later. Perhaps he ate one of those cakes.

The end of the line (or maybe the beginning - let's just call it the terminus) is a place where everyone is

      Living
       In
        Vain
         Expectation
         Regarding
         Pay-
        Out
        On
          Lottery

Scousers *are* very lucky. They have a football team who are

      Lionhearts
      In
       Victory...
       Eleven
        Reds...
        Pride
        Of
        Our
         Land

and a racecourse where:

   Great
    Runners
     Alongside
      Nags,
       Dashing

      Nine
       Abreast,
      Thrill
       Insistent
        Onlookers :
       Noblest
       And
        Lowliest

And where do Scousers go on their holidays? Well nowadays Mallorca or Lanzarote, but I'm sure those of you old enough can still spend time

    Remembering
    Holidays
    You
     Loved

It sounds idyllic but I suspect it's wet, windy and the tea's weak.

Should you prefer a trip to the mountains rather than the seaside, you can take an ickle-wickle train to the

      Summit
       Nursery
        Of
         Welsh
          Dragons
           Overlooking
           Nant Peris

Or if a total escape to another country is more appealing, then

      Hearing
      Of
       Leprechauns
       You
        Head
         Emerald-Isle-wards
          Asking
           Directions

Heading south now along the Welsh coast, we encounter a

    Picturesque
    Old
     Railway
     Town
      Hiding
     Mad
      Angry
     Dog
     On
      Guard-duty

The train was used to carry the slate down from the hills and to the ships waiting in the harbour. I like the fact that one of the wettest parts of Britain provides the best roofing material.

Meanwhile, Edward the First must have been

   Having
  A
   Royal
    Laugh
     Erecting
    Castle
    Here

I mean, why? It doesn't do anything. By the time you've reached here you've conquered the whole of Wales anyway!

Leaving vast tracts of Wales unexplored, we whizz off to the south, thinking interesting thoughts such as

> **S**ome
> **W**omen
>   **A**thletes
> **N**eed
>   **S**having
>   **E**very
>   **A**fternoon

while passing through places where there's

> **N**ot
> **E**ven
> **A**
>   **T**oilet
>   **H**ere

in which to test the theory that

      Creamed
       Asparagus
        Reduces
         Dryness
          In
           Frigid
            Fannies

At the exit from Wales, just before you reach the Severn Bridge (it's free to get out but you have to pay to get back in), is a town which shares its name with many others in the land. In fact, in my road atlas there are ten entries with this name, plus these two:

      Numbering
       Eleven
        With
         Pagnell ;
          On-Tay
           Registers
            Twelfth

By the way, Caerleon was the "old port", but it was too shallow for the bigger ships to reach, so this "new port" was built.

Back into England, we meander north once more, into the bosom of the countryside where we can

    Heartily
     Eat
      Ruminants'
     Entrails
    For
     Our
      Roast
       Dinners

This is also the home of Bulmers cider. Percy Bulmer founded the company in Hereford in 1887. In the first year he produced 4000 gallons. Today this figure is "5 million hectolitres" (thank you to the Bulmers website).

To translate this into something that makes sense, a hectolitre is 100 litres and there are roughly 5 litres in a gallon so it equates to 100 million gallons, or 200 Olympic swimming pools.

A brief excursion back into the Midlands to some towns we skirted past earlier, brings us to the area which takes credit for originating civil engineering using iron rather than wood and masonry.

> **T**homas
>   **E**ngineers
>   **L**ofty
>   **F**rameworks
>   **O**ver
>   **R**olling
>   **D**ales

Thomas Telford was actually Scottish - he was a great engineer and did a lot of his work in the Shropshire area, especially on structures for the canal network.

The "iron" thing was initiated by Abraham Darby who found a way of producing it in large quantities using coal instead of charcoal. This was in the pertinently named Coalbrookdale in 1709. In 1779 his grandson built the first iron bridge in the world. This was in the even more pertinently named Ironbridge. Why did it take 70 years from improving the iron-making process to building the bridge? And then another 120 years until Frank Hornby invented Meccano? Surely it would have been better to invent

Meccano first, then they could have built a model of the bridge to check that it worked.

Another scene of industrialisation, this time of the transport variety, grew a whole town around it. Ask anyone who remembers (there aren't many left now) and they'll tell you

    Cleaning
    Railway
    Engines
    Wasn't
    Easy

Crewe was also the home of Rolls Royce

    Chauffeured
    Rollers
    Epitomise
    Well-heeled
    Executives

Apparently Bentleys are still made here, but not Rollers any more. Both Bentley and Rolls Royce made aircraft engines, Bentleys powering the Sopwith Camel of the First World War and Rolls Royce the Spitfires and Hurricanes of the Second. The irony here is that Bentley is now owned by Volkswagen and Rolls Royce (cars) is owned by BMW.

A few hundred years before all the hustle and bustle of first the steam age and then the motor age, there was a place just down the road where you could

    Sample
     The
      Oven-ready
     Kaolin
      Experience

Potteries sprung up by their dozen in and around Stoke, and gave their name to a whole region.

And to the south there is another famous pottery, where they also happened to revel in a recipe for a tangy taste. In fact,

    What
   Other
    Run-of-the-mill
   City
    Enjoys
     Saucy
      Taste
       Everyone
        Relishes **?**

In 1838 the first bottles of "Lea & Perrins Worcestershire Sauce" hit the grocers' shops. It was based on a recipe brought back from India by Sir Charles Sandys, Chief Justice of that country. Both the sauce and Lea & Perrins are still going strong.

Now to a posh horse racing town with two famous colleges, one for boys and one

   Containing
   Highly
    Educated
    Ladies
     There,
    Every
    Night
    Has
    A
     Mare

but, unfortunately for the ladies, no stallion.

Before bumping into the M4, we come to God's Wonderful Railway (GWR) where

  Steam
   Whistles
  Into
   Night -
    Diesels
   Only
    Now

Brunel's Great Western mainline, on its way to the west, passes through some ancient towns, one of which lived up to its name for centuries. Often must have been heard the cry of

    Bring
    A
     Towel
      Horace **!!!**

or Harriet or whatever the slave happened to be called.

Rhyming slang is always fun, so forgive me for pointing out that the original terminus of the Great Western also happens to be a

    Big
     Round
      Item
       Sucked
        Tenderly
       Or
        Licked

Bristol has two league football teams: City and Rovers. No one seems to have come up with an amusing rhyme for Rovers - any offers?

Hitting the coast again, this place was once a haven for coachloads of holidaymakers. It now seems a trifle run-down (perhaps the coaches didn't stop - ho ho) but it is still a

    Wholly
   Enjoyable
  Seaside
   Town,
     Overlooking
     Notoriously

      Seedy
     Undermined
    Pier / eer,
     Entertaining
      Revellers &

      Mediocre
     Authors
      Requiring
       Excitement

Weston-Super-Mare has a pier and a peer - one is a large erection, the other is a prick.

You can read the above either way. Oh my Lord!!

Our next stop is a hill (or, in these parts, a tor) although at 518 feet high it is barely more than a bump (I reckon it's about a C-cup - see BRISTOL). Anyway, more importantly, King Arthur decided to hold meetings here. Nowadays, a whole bunch of people hold a meeting every summer (with the odd hiatus) in a field where you can

>
> **G**et
> **L**aid
> **A**nd
> **S**ee
> **T**ons
> **O**f
> **N**ew
> **B**ands
> **U**nder
> **R**ainfall
> **Y**early

It's my idea of hell (the muddy field that is, not the music). Why use a nice comfy toilet when you can drive 300 miles and crap in a hedge?

Now we'll visit the heart of a moor, a picturesque place indeed, but lacking a decent pub - there's just a hotel and a café. For that reason, the locals spend more time than they should in their wellies, skulking around where

    Silhouetted
   In
    Moorland,
   Our
    Nice
     Sheep
      Behave
       Attractively
      Towards
       Holidaymakers

Exmoor is one of my favourite places. Exford (the next village along from Simonsbath) is a great place for a pint of Exmoor Gold in the White Horse. Dunkery Beacon, the highest point on Exmoor, is ideal for walkers who don't like walking because it's only about a mile from the car park and you can return to the hotel and brag that you've climbed - yes - you've got it - the highest point on Exmoor.

Where Exmoor drops, almost vertically, into the sea is my very favourite place, where in 1899 there was a

    Lifeboat
    Yanked
    Nocturnally
    Moor-wards
    Overland
    Unto
    The
    Harbour

In that last year of the 19th century the tide conditions made launching the Lynmouth lifeboat from its home port impossible, so the crew and locals, assisted by many many horses, lugged it up to the top of Exmoor (via Countisbury Hill) and back down again (the infamous Porlock Hill) to launch at Porlock. It accomplished its mission of rescuing survivors from a foundering ship, but could not return because of the wind conditions and the crew had to make for the Welsh coast and shelter there until the weather improved.

Another seaside town has

      Isolated
      Lagoons
      Fronting
      Rocks
      And
        Coves
         Offering
         Magical
         Bathing
         Experience

I drove through Ilfracombe for years without stopping there. It always looked like it needed a coat of paint, and much of it still does. But take a walk through the cold tunnels carved through solid rock and out onto Ilfracombe's sun-trapping beaches with their man-made lagoons where children may safely splash and play - it's bliss!

All the roads round here lead to one place, which is a shame because it is a

    Beautiful
   Area
    Ruined
     Negotiating
     Stuck
      Traffic -
     A
       Phenomenally
      Leisurely
       Experience

It's at long last got its bypass.

Off to Cornwall now, England's outpost, and the middle of another moor where you have to

   Beware
  Of
   Danger -
  Murderous
  Inn
   Nearby

Actually the three moors around here, Dartmoor, Exmoor and Bodmin are lumps of hard granite which have remained steadfastly high and uneroded while all around has dissolved in the rains of time. They stick out like the spines on a stickleback, and when you get to the sea they're not finished yet because the next set of spines which pierce the surface are the Isles of Scilly.

The coast here is surfers' paradise, but unfortunately without the Antipodean weather. Surfing has become so popular that there's no room left on the beach for toddlers with buckets and spades. It must be that the

> **N**ever
>   **E**nding
>   **W**aves
>   **Q**uench
>   **U**nfulfilled
>   **A**dult
>   **Y**earnings

Regarding the British weather, allegedly it's warming up! We can look out to sea and say to each other

"**L**ook :
  A
    Nice
     Deadly
    Shark

     Enjoying
      Nutritious
       Dippers**!**"

- "I've never seen that before!"

Apparently a "Great White" was spotted off Cornwall. No doubt some do-gooder will slaughter it. Personally I think they should leave it as it will make watching the surfers more fun as they try to escape its razor-sharp teeth.

From Land's End, if you are high enough to see out to sea for 28 miles and it's not raining or foggy, you can see

    Seductive
   Crystal
  Islands
   Luring
    Landlubbers
     Yonder

Between Land's End and Scilly is the sunken land of Lyonesse. If King Arthur should ever return, Lyonesse will rise from the depths. You then won't be able to see Scilly, not because of the island in between, but because of all the tourists.

On 9th May 1904, City of

>**T**rain
>　**R**eaches
>　　**U**ltimate
>　　**R**apidity
>　　　**O**verland

was the first in the world (possibly) to exceed 100 miles per hour, without falling off a bridge (see DUNDEE). It accomplished this feat (according to the person who timed it - Charles Rous-Marten) for the distance between two quarter-mile posts (so that'll be a quarter of a mile) descending the 1 in 80 Wellington Bank near Taunton (so as I couldn't find a way of getting cider into the equation, TAUNTON should be "Train Achieves Uniquely Notable TON").

It's pretty around here. On the south coast you can

>   **L**ive
>   **O**n
>   **O**cean
>   **E**nchantment

While along the coast, as Drake played bowls, the

>   **P**irates
>   **L**ured
>   **Y**our
>   **M**other-in-law
>   **O**ut
>   **U**nto
>   **T**he
>   **H**amoaze

She was only young then – remember that Sir Francis Drake was a pirate and enjoyed a quiet game of bowls on the Hoe whilst keeping an eye out across the Hamoaze (the name of the bit of water where the rivers enter Plymouth Sound) for any Spanish ships on the horizon.

Following the south coast for quite a long way, we arrive at the home of the eightysomethings, where

      Battalions
       Of
        Undertakers
         Ram-raid
          Newcomer
           Embalmers,
          Making
         Off
          Using
           Their
            Hearses

The lucrative Bournemouth undertaking trade must have its "turf wars".

Bournemouth was invented by Lewis Tregonwell as recently as 1810. I suppose he must have retired there to get away from all the other senior citizens. Not, as occurs nowadays, to join them.

A quick foray inland brings us to somewhere older (well older than the place, if not the people). On a plain near here is where some

Smart
  Alec
    Liked
      Implanting
        Stones,
          Bamboozling
            Unsuspecting
              Researchers
                Yet

My theory is that Stonehenge was a "student teaching kit" for a trainee dinosaur dentist. What do you reckon?

Titanic last docked in this place, then

  Sailed
    Off
      Until
        The
          Horizon
            Appeared
              Mauvey-
            Pink
          To
            Orangey
          Night

A poetic end to a tragic trip:
Into the icy waters we slip.

Across the Solent now and could these be

> **C**attle?
> **O**r
>   **W**ickedly
>   **E**xpensive
>   **S**howboats?

The only cows in Cowes carry handbags (made of cows).

Just upstream there are more

> **C**aptains
> **H**aving
> **I**nebriated
> **C**ruising
> **H**olidays.
> **E**lderly
> **S**pouses
> **T**anning
> **E**very
> **'R**inkle

Luckily, we're soon in "Pompey" where

    Pamela
   Offers
    Relaxation
    To
     Sailors
     Most
      Often
       Using
       The
        Harbour

She's been doing it since her Gran retired.

Next up among these south coast dens of iniquity is another coffin-dodgers' paradise full of

   Wrinkled
  Old
   Relics
    Tossing
     Hedge-clippings
     Into
      Neighbours'
      Gardens

If your preference is for a shingly beach, get whatever rocks you with some

    Brief
     Relationships
    In
      Gay
       Home
        Town
       Of
        Naturism

If your boyfriend dumps you and you're feeling depressed, get in the car and head east to where

    Before
     Experiencing
    A
     Cliff-
      Hanger,
     Your

       Handbrake
       Exhibits
      A
       Defect

If you find you lack the courage for four-wheel free-fall, there's always a relaxing break to be had at one of the south coast's friendly guest houses. Look in the local papers for an advert along the lines of:

    Ethel
   Andrews
  Seeks
   Teetotal
    Boarders
    Of
     Unblemished
      Reputation -
    No
     Eating

(in your room). Geographically speaking, this part of England is the nearest to France. In 1066 this juxtaposition had a drawback when there was an

   Historical
  Altercation
  Serving
  To
   Illustrate
    Norman's
   Great
    Superiority

In fact, if there were newspapers around at that time, the headlines could be succinctly put thus:

    Harold.
     Arrow.
      Straight
       Through
      'Is
        New
         Glasses.
          Surrender!

Later, after the French had settled in (actually Normans weren't really French - they were North-men, or Vikings, but we won't split hairs) there was a chap who fancied some dinner but didn't want to break off from his game of cribbage just for the inconvenience of eating it. So instead of calling for his "pipe and his bowl", he called for something

    Sliced
    And
     Nice,
      Devoured
     Without
       Interrupting
      Card
       Hand

and *it* was called after him.

Sadly, the Earl of Sandwich probably never even set foot in the town sharing his name, but never mind, it's a good job he wasn't called the Earl of Snotburger.

When the Normans invaded, they probably landed about 7000 people and managed to take over the whole country. Nowadays, considerably more

Desperate
Overseas
Visitors
Enter
Regardless

I'd rather go to a place where the girls spend

Winter -
Huddled
In
Tights.
Summer -
Tits
And
Bare
Legs
Everywhere

I wonder what Whitstable's really like? Famed for its oysters, it is also one end of the (extinct) Canterbury and Whitstable railway which was the first to use locomotive steam power to convey passengers in regular service (see STOCKTON). It was known to locals as the "Crab and Winkle Line" after the initial letters of the two termini.

The locomotive used was Invicta which stood outside in the rain for a hundred years in Canterbury where:

    Cathedrals
     Are
      Nice
       To
        Explore ;
       Rubbing
        Brasses
         Unwinds
        Rowdy
         Youngsters

before some kind souls felt sorry for it and gave it a new home in Canterbury's museum.

Some places are of no note whatsoever. Now that we're in the home counties, we shall meet a lot of them. To start with, we encounter a town just like all others of its ilk where

    All
     Southerners
      Harbour
       Fears
        Of
         Rivals'
          Diesel 4x4s

Sad is the word. Read on - it gets sadder.

Remember this?

    Since
     Eighty-seven,
      Various
       Estimates
        Number
         One-oak
          After
           Killer
            Storm

Have they planted six new ones?

Back in the 40s, the young lads were jumping in their crates and firing up their Rolls Royce engines (see CREWE).

    Before
    I
      Go
        Gallantly
          Intercepting
        Nazi

        Hordes
        I
          Loop-the-
          Loop

Getting near to London now so it's getting busy. Most are trying to escape by

    Going
      Abroad
        To
          Wherever
            It's
              Cheapest...
                Knockout **!!!**

If you lived in an

> **E**nvironment
> **L**ost
> **T**o
> **H**oodies
> **A**nd
> **M**uggers

you'd definitely try and leave. Belmarsh is where most of the residents move to. Alternatively you could

> **C**rap
> **R**ight
> **O**n
> **Y**our
> **D**oorstep ;
> **O**r
> **N**earer !

I feel I may be being unkind, but I can't help it.

We're in Surrey now. The sound of this place

>   **D**eserves
>   **O**de
>   **R**hyming
>   **"K**nob"...
>   **I**
>   **N**ominate
>   **"G**ob"

Well - I always thought Dorking was a noun not a town - just sounds rude doesn't it? I suppose it could also be a verb - have you ever been dorked?

Whereas this place is absolutely chocker with

>   **E**xecutives
>   **S**eeking
>   **H**ard-
>   **E**arned
>   **R**etirement

My brother lived there...... then he retired.

Just up the road a bit

>
> **W**omen
> **I**magine
> **M**en's
> **B**alls
> **L**obbing
> **E**ntrancingly,
> **D**ipping
> **O**ver
> **N**et

Tennis, strawberries, girls that grunt, men that wax, all mixed together - and nowadays all the players are really boring - who gives a ...?

Also near here we can enter a

> **K**aleidoscopic
> **E**vergreen
> **W**orld

where we must

> **K**eep
> **E**verything
> **W**atered

but it's all a bit depressing when you're rubbish at gardening like me. Perhaps I should get one of the those plants that only flowers once every seven years - that way it'll be ages before anyone notices whether it's dead or not.

They're a bit hot on horse-racing round these Surrey parts, what with Sandown Park and Kempton Park, this is a great part of the world for an

  Exhilarating
  Pastime
  Seated
  On
  Mount

Ahhh, Surrey...

  Guide
   Us
   In
    Life's
    Destiny
     For
     Opportunism
      Rarely
      Delivers

I hate it...

Let's leave and go to somewhere else. But is it better?

    Ridiculously
    Expensive
      Accountants'
     Dormitory -
    Imagine
    Nothing
     Ghastlier

No.

But it can be a bit Royal around here. Ask the grandchildren and they'll tell you

   "**W**hat
    If
     Nanny
     Does
      Sign
      Off
       '**R**egina' ?"

But She won't be home because She'll be mooching about in designer wellies while her subjects are busy

Arranging
  Stuffed
    Cockatoos
   On
     Titfers

For, you see, Royal Ascot is noted for its many posh hats with extinct-dead birds on top of them, and brain-dead birds beneath them.

Heading townwards, we pass through a place where once there were made

  Standard
   Omnibuses,
    Unceasingly
     Transporting
    Hoi polloi
    Around
      London's
     Lanes

Southall used to be the home of the AEC factory which manufactured nearly all of London's buses, including the iconic RT and the Routemaster. Now they've been replaced by foreign things with no padding on the seats, and there's no heating until the engine catches fire (which they do - regularly).

We'll head off to the East End now and use our imaginations. It's dark, it's 1888, it's the weekend - there's a stranger about looking for excitement - but who is he? I quote the following extract from his curriculum vitae:

    Worthwhile
    Hobbies
     I
      Truly
       Enjoy:
        Carving
         Harlots'
          Abdomens,
         Penning
          Enigmatic
         Letters

Could it be: Jack the Ripper? A man who used to

    Live
    Our
     Nightlife,
     Dream
     Our
      Nightlife

While a certain bell was

    Banging
     Its
      Gong

         Bonggggggggg !
        Every
         Night-long

This is one of those mysteries with no ending. It is best

    Left
     O
      N
       D
      O
       N

Left "undone"... Sorry.

Now for some sport. After spending some quality time by the Thames watching

    Two
     Hues,
      Equally

Blue,
Oxford
Await
Their

Rivals,
A
Cambridge
Eight

we shall sample some football clubs.

In the East there is a set of supporters who can proudly declare

We're
England's
Strongest
Team

Hard
And
Mean

just because Moore, Hurst and Peters were captain and goal-scorers in the 1966 world cup final.

In the West there is a place where a

      Club
     Homing
       Expensive
     Louts
        Stimulates
         Everyone's
        Animosity

or

     Champion
    Heroes
     Evermore...
    Loyal
     Supporters
     Ever
      Adore

depending on your viewpoint and allegiance.

Heading out of London to the North, we meet two rival football clubs:

a
    Team
    Of
      Titans...
     The
      English
      Nation's
      High
      And
        Mighty-ans...

and an
    Amazing
    Red
    Side...
      England's
      Noblest
      And
        London's-pride

and a football stadium

    Where
    England
    Mostly
    Bloody
    Lose
     Every
     Year

North of London, in the suburbs, while

    Cycling
     Home,
      Erica
       Snags
        Her
         Underwear
          Negotiating
           Traffic-calming

Some places take your breath away! I mean...

    What
    A
     Thoroughly
     Flipping
    'Orrible
      Rotten
       Dump !

This is

    Rather
    A
     Dull
      Life -
       Expect
        Tittle-
         Tattle

Some places in the Home Counties offer a

>   **H**ostile
>   **E**nvironment
>   **R**epellent
>   **T**o
>   **F**oreigners
>   **O**f
>   **R**egional
>   **D**escent

A little further north is a place which is famous for two things - hats (which it no longer makes)

>   **L**urking
>   **U**nder
>   **T**op-hat :
>   **O**nly
>   **N**its

and an airport (which is thriving)

>   **L**ift
>   **U**ndercarriage...
>   **T**ake
>   **O**ff...
>   **N**early-made-it !!

Ooops! What a cock-up.

But not as bad as our next stop, the cock-up that reinvented the word.

    Must
     It
      Look
       Tacky **?**
      Orderly
      Neat

       Kennels
        Expanding
       Yonder **:**
      North
      East
       South

The land of a thousand roundabouts, all leading to another road which looked exactly like the last, and all sending you where you don't want to go.

Now for some complete cobblers.

    Niffy
    Old
     Rotten
      Trainers
     Have
      Attacked
     My
      Patent-leather
      Thigh-boots
     Over-
     Night

Impossible to get footwear into Northampton. "One out of ten" - could do better.

Other Northamptonshire towns were also in the same trade, but now I'm sad to say that

    Really
   Useful
    Shoes
    Have
     Deserted
    East
     Northamptonshire

Crossing into a different county now, we arrive at the place where was written the first "best-seller" (well maybe). It was a place where

    Bunyan
     Enjoyed
    Daily
     Feast
      Of
       Religious
        Dreaming

and converted this into an incredibly popular allegorical tale for the masses. Well, the masses that could read, which wasn't very many.

A more modern epigram would be

    Breast
     Enlargement...
      Defiantly
       Firm
        Or
         Rather
          Droopy**?**

County hopping again, we find a place which has a

> **R**iddle
>   **O**f
>   **Y**awning
>   **S**ubterranean
>   **T**unnels,
>   **O**ddly
>   **N**eglected

Few people are aware of Royston's secret cave hidden beneath the junction of Ermine Street and Icknield Way. Decorated with both Pagan and Christian images, it defies explanation,

whereas

> **R**iding
> **O**n
>   **Y**oung
>   **S**caffolders
>   **T**urns
>   **O**n
>   **N**icole

does not.

All around here, we find places where

      Blatantly
     Indulgent
       Southerners,
     Highly
      Overpaid,
       Purposely
      Spoil

           Sex-mad
           Truculent
           Offspring
           Rather
           Than
           Face-down
           Obscenely
           Ranting
           Daughters

much like every other affluent town in Southern England.

Once again, we arrive at a place of escape:

    "Standstill-airport**"** :
     Take
     All
      Night
       Struggling
      To
        Escape
        Drizzle

Still, it's better than staying somewhere

      Housing
     A
      Right
     Load
     Of
       Wheeler-dealers

You can almost smell those

    Hairy
     Armpits
      Requiring
     Lots
      Of
       Washing

Essex is great. It's got

    Boy
     Racers
      Attracting
       Impressionable
      Nubile
       Teenagers
       Revving
        Engines
        Endlessly

these being "Essex Girls". The alternative to flying out of Stansted is London's own seaside, "the Cockney's paradise", where the townies once flocked in their thousands. They even built a pier to stick out into the Thames so that the holidaymakers could arrive by boat (before the age of trains). The problem always was whether to take

    Sun-hats
   Or
    Umbrellas ?
    Take
     Hats.
      Expect
       Non-stop
      Drizzle

A solution to this predicament was provided by Billy Butlin. He decided that, when the weather was inclement, you should be able to pursue lots of amusements (other than the obvious) indoors:

    Campers,
   Laughing
  And
   Canoodling,
   Thrive
  On
   'Nobbliest

  Of
  'Nees

    Sessions
   Every
    Afternoon

The second Butlins holiday camp was set up in Clacton on Sea. The first was at Skegness.

The Clacton site is now a housing estate. Skeggie is still going strong.

When those "knobbly knees" no longer work and the rheumatism sets in, you are

>**F**acing
>>**R**etirement
>>>**I**n
>>>>**N**atural
>>>>>**T**ime-warp
>>>>>>**O**f
>>>>>>>**N**ostalgia

Frinton-on-sea - the perfect place to see out the last of one's days, with

>**F**rugally
>>**R**ationed
>>>**I**ncontinence
>>>>**N**appies
>>>>>**T**o
>>>>>>**O**ver-
>>>>>>>**N**ineties

Remember the old saying "Harwich for the Continent, Frinton for the incontinent"? No? (You can't remember anything any more, can you... ?)

Talking of the Continent,

    Hitching
   A
    Ride
     With
      International
       Container
        Haulage

is becoming a popular exploit. Everything arrives on lorries nowadays - watch out for the ones with breathing holes punched in the sides.

We're nearly at the end of our trip now, on the last leg back to where we started. That is if we can make it along the coast, past the

    Standard
    Inhabitants :
    Zero
     Eyes
      With
       Eleven
        Luminous
         Legs

This is the "nuclear" family.

~~We~~ have one more seaside resort to which we ~~can~~ resort. And it has its endearing features:

> **Y**oung
> **A**nd
> **R**andy
> **M**aidens
> **O**ffer
> **U**p
> **T**heir
> **H**avens

Also known as Yarmuff, it's a great place - "Kiss me ~~quiekm~~".

Which rather makes the impassioned order

> **'N**ickers
> **O**ff
> **R**eady
> **W**hen
> **I**
> **C**ome
> **H**ome

Completely superfluous! I hope you had fun.

Another great book from Luvbutton Press

The Effing A Cup

by *Ron Accrington* (the greatest football manager in relegation history !!!)
ISBN 978-0-9557635-1-9

This story is about **FOOTBALL**.

> The little town of Hetherington Sidney are drawn against the mighty Jam Utd in the 3rd round of the FA Cup.

This story is about **POLITICS**.

> Stan Dovehawk is the Labour candidate for Hetherington Sidney in the forthcoming local by-election.

This story is about **SEX**.

> Hetherington's star player, Sean Shagdit is dating the delightfully pretty and aristocratic super-model, Lady Fiona Opiumden; but he's too drunk to notice her most of the time. She finds Dovehawk more attentive to her womanly needs, and his ruthless ambition exciting.

> Add in Jam Utd's trip to Brazil for the World Sex Championships and Dovehawk being ousted as Labour candidate by the Women's Committee, and you're in for an hilarious non-stop treat…

Forthcoming title from Luvbutton Press

The Spanking Good Diet

by *Jasmine Cliff*
ISBN 978-0-9557635-2-6

Learn how to lose weight by eating slap-up meals, like:
- strapping sausages…
- tanned baked beans…
- thrashed potato…
- whipped custard…
- belting good banoffee pie…
- walloping waffles…
- beaten egg caramels…
- celery and carrot canes…

And if you put on a pound?

Gently rub some delicious ice-cold raspberry coulis onto that sore sore spanked bottom…

Contains the most outstanding recipes to revolutionise your relationship between you, your partner and your weight.

So exciting you won't be able to put it down, or sit down, for a week!